Welcome to Ready for Reading

Toronto Public Library wants all children to get off to a great start in life. It is never too early to start reading with your child!

As your child's first teacher, the few minutes you spend reading together each day lay the foundation for a love of reading that will last a lifetime. It's also a wonderful way to spend close and happy times together.

Toronto Public Library is very pleased to be able to offer this unique resource to help parents, caregivers and children get started on their reading adventures together. We have gathered a selection of rhymes, activities, favourite books and more, to show you how fun and easy it can be to help children build the important skills they need to get ready for reading and for success in school.

Open the guide to any page and you will find useful information that you can immediately put into practice. Feel free to hop, skip or jump your way through. Or, if you prefer to read it cover to cover, that's okay too. Our hope is that this guide will support you and your family and help you understand the many benefits of talking, reading, singing, playing and writing with your child.

Remember, at the library we are always here to help. If you have any questions, just ask.

Jane Pyper

Jane Pyper
City Librarian

Ready for Reading

As parents and caregivers, you are your child's first and best teachers, and home is where your child begins to learn.

★ You play a key role in your child's early literacy development because you can encourage her in ways that no one else can.

★ Each child is unique and you know your child best. Make the most of playful learning opportunities in your everyday life.

★ When you read, talk and play together, you help develop your child's knowledge about reading and writing before he can actually read and write. So, read together as often as possible to ensure your child's success in school and beyond.

★ It's never too early to start. It's never too late to learn more. And your child will develop these skills no matter what language you speak at home.

EVERYDAY ACTIVITIES BUILD SKILLS
TALK · READ · SING · PLAY · WRITE

Table of contents

I LIKE BOOKS!

Print motivation

Children who enjoy books will want to learn to read

★ Enjoying books together every day is the first step toward developing a love of reading. Start the day your child is born.

★ Positive, fun and playful experiences with books and stories foster a desire to read and encourage your child to keep trying to read.

★ This chapter offers some ideas and activities to help you give your child a love of books.

Action rhymes

Children love rhymes with actions.

ZOOM, ZOOM, ZOOM

Here's a rhyme that you can do with any child. Gently bounce or rock your baby and lift her into the air at "Blast off." Older children can learn to follow the actions.

Zoom, zoom, zoom,	*(Standing, rub hands upward)*
We're going to the moon.	*(Point up into the sky)*
Zoom, zoom, zoom,	*(Standing, rub hands upward)*
We're going to the moon.	*(Point up into the sky)*
If you want to take a trip,	
Climb aboard my rocket ship.	*(Pretend to climb a ladder)*
Zoom, zoom, zoom,	*(Standing, rub hands upward)*
We're going to the moon.	
10, 9, 8, 7, 6, 5, 4, 3, 2, 1,	*(Slowly crouch down)*
Blast off!!!	*(Jump up!)*

 ONLINE VIDEO

Visit **torontopubliclibrary.ca/readyforreading** to view a video performance of fun rhymes like this one.

Developmental milestones

Each child is unique, but you may observe these signs that your child is interested in language, books and reading.

Babies:

★ Respond to your voice and facial expressions

★ Start to look at picture books with interest and try pointing to objects

Toddlers:

★ May pretend to read books themselves

★ Begin to understand how to handle books

Preschoolers:

★ Enjoy listening to and talking about storybooks

★ Make attempts to read and write.

DID YOU KNOW?
A child's interest in reading is an important predictor of later reading achievement.

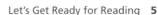

Go Away, Big Green Monster!
Ed Emberley, 1992
This book uses simple shapes and bright colours. Each page features a new part of a big green monster, which then disappears one part at a time as the children command it to go away.

Have fun reading!

Bring a sense of adventure to your reading. Read with humour, expression and enthusiasm.

★ Give the story characters different voices. Make your voice loud or soft, high or low. Read faster or slower to fit the story, and add pauses for dramatic effect. Play with adding sounds.

★ Try using a puppet or stuffed animal to help read or tell a story.

★ Involve the whole family in stories.

❋ I Like to Play
🍁 Marla Stewart Konrad, 2010
Children from all over the world are shown playing in gorgeous colour photographs. What games do you and your child like to play together?

Red is Best
🍁 Kathy Stinson, 1982
Illus. Robin Baird Lewis
No one understands the perfection of red like this little girl.

❋ This symbol identifies Toronto Public Library's top annual picks of Canadian children's books for building reading readiness. Because the first books you share with your child should also be the best! See pages 52-53. Learn more at **torontopubliclibrary.ca/readyforreading**

Language is fun

Songs and rhymes are playful ways to make language and learning fun.

TOMMY THUMBS

Have your child copy your actions.

Tommy Thumbs are up,	*(Wiggle thumbs up)*
And Tommy Thumbs are down.	*(Wiggle thumbs down)*
Tommy Thumbs are dancing all around the town.	*(Wiggle Thumbs)*
Dance them on your shoulders,	*(Tap thumbs on shoulders)*
Dance them on your head.	*(Tap thumbs on head)*
Dance them on your knees,	*(Tap thumbs on knees)*
And tuck them into bed.	*(Hide thumbs in fists)*

OPEN THEM, SHUT THEM

Open them, shut them,
Open them, shut them,
Give a little clap, clap, clap.
Open them, shut them,
Open them, shut them,
Put them in your lap, lap, lap.
Creep them, creep them,
Creep them, creep them,
Right up to your chin, chin, chin.
Open wide your little mouth…
But do not put them in!

Start a conversation

One way to engage your child in a book is to start a conversation about what you're reading.

★ Relate the pictures and the story to your child's own experiences. For example: "What happened when we went to the park?"

★ Talk about what the characters are doing or feeling.

★ Share a book together without actually reading it.

DID YOU KNOW?
Playing is how children learn. Share with your child all the wonderful rhymes, books and songs your parents shared with you as a child in your home language.

Make reading time special

Sharing a book is an opportunity to bond with your child and to show him that reading is important.

★ Find a cosy place to read and, if possible, read with your child in your lap, or sit close and cuddle. Being close makes reading together a warm and happy experience that your child looks forward to.

★ Tell your child how reading with him is the favourite part of your day.

★ Remember to smile at your child while you are reading.

Play peek-a-boo games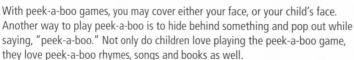

With peek-a-boo games, you may cover either your face, or your child's face. Another way to play peek-a-boo is to hide behind something and pop out while saying, "peek-a-boo." Not only do children love playing the peek-a-boo game, they love peek-a-boo rhymes, songs and books as well.

PEEK-A-BOO SONG
Sing to the tune of "Frère Jacques."

Peek-a-boo! Peek-a-boo!   *(Cover face with hands)*
I see you! I see you!   *(Open hands to uncover face)*
I see your button nose.   *(Point to your nose or child's nose)*
I see your tiny toes.   *(Point to child's feet)*
I see you. Peek-a-boo!   *(Cover and uncover face)*

Personalize this rhyme by using your child's name in place of "you."

Peek-a-Moo!
Marie Torres Cimarusti, 1998
Illus. Stephanie Peterson
Play peek-a-boo with farm animals.

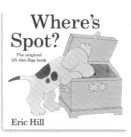

Where's Spot?
Eric Hill, 1980
This lift-the-flap book follows Sally, the mother, as she searches the house for little pup Spot.

Actual Size
Steve Jenkins, 2004
This engaging non-fiction book introduces children to some of the wonders of our natural world.

How to choose books your child will love

It's not surprising that children will love to read if they love what they're reading. Here are suggestions for how to choose books your child will love:

★ Follow your child's developing interests. Share picture books, information books and true stories with your child.

★ Ask your public librarian to help you find books on the subject your child is interested in. It's a chance for you and your child to learn together.

★ Let your child choose her own books and stories to read, to borrow from the library, or to buy.

★ Books with cut-outs, lift-the-flaps, pop-ups or anything that moves are favourites. Kids love them! Look for touch-and-feel features, scratch-and-sniff elements and sounds.

★ For babies, board books are sturdier and more durable. They tend to be small and easy to handle by small hands. Cloth books, as well as those with a mirror, can also be good choices for babies.

Make your own books. Make them personal.

★ Children love hearing stories about when you were a child. Create a photo album of people that your child knows. Share stories with your child about the people in the pictures.

★ To create a book on a subject that interests your child, start by collecting pictures from old magazines, advertisements or newspapers.

★ If possible, let your child choose the pictures and help cut them out. Your child can help sort them and glue them onto sheets of paper.

★ Label the pictures and make a cover sheet for the book's title. Staple the pages together and let your child tell you stories about the pictures in his book.

Over and over again!

Young children love repetition and learn from it. Repeated readings are comforting and build self-confidence. Children are more likely to try to read a book on their own when they are already familiar with the story.

FIVE LITTLE MONKEYS JUMPING ON THE BED

Five little monkeys jumping on the bed,

(Hold up five fingers and move hand up and down)

One fell off and bumped his head!

(Rub head with hand)

Momma called the doctor and the doctor said,

"No more monkeys jumping on the bed."

(Point index finger and move it back and forth)

Repeat rhyme for:

Four little monkeys…

Three little monkeys…

Two little monkeys…

One little monkey…

Momma called the doctor and the doctor said,

"No more monkeys jumping on the bed."

(Point index finger and move it back and forth)

A popular book version of this little finger play by Eileen Christelow is available through your local library branch.

Read every day

Share books with your child, even your baby, every day and throughout the day.

★ It's helpful to create a special time for reading, such as after dinner, before naps or at bedtime. Make books and stories a part of your child's daily routine.

★ Read together when you are both in a good mood. Reading happily even for a short time will help develop your child's interest in reading.

Ten Little Fingers and Ten Little Toes
Mem Fox, 2008
Illus. Helen Oxenbury
This delightful book celebrates a world of adorable babies.

Bear Snores On
Karma Wilson, 2002
Illus. Jane Chapman
Bear sleeps while more and more animals enter his cave to escape the cold weather outside. He's missing all the fun!

Singing together

Singing is a fun way to make language come alive for you and your child, and the music makes the words easier to remember. A much-loved song for children of all ages is:

IF YOU'RE HAPPY AND YOU KNOW IT

Have your child copy your actions.

If you're happy and you know it, clap your hands.　　(*Clap hands*)
If you're happy and you know it, clap your hands.　　(*Clap hands*)
If you're happy and you know it,
And you really want to show it,
If you're happy and you know it, clap your hands.　　(*Clap hands*)
Other verses:
… stamp your feet.　　　　　(*Stamp feet*)
… shout "hooray!"　　　　　(*Raise arms above head*)

When you sing at home, have fun making up your own variations. As your child gets older, let her make up her own new verses, too.

"…touch your nose…"
"If you're sad and you know it, cry boo-hoo…"
"If you're dirty and you know it, take a bath…"
"If you're tired and you know it, go to sleep…"

YOUR TURN!

Answer these together

Who reads to me?

Where do I like to read books?

When do I like to read books?

What is my mom's favourite book?

What is my dad's favourite book?

What is my favourite book?

What is my favourite book about?

DID YOU KNOW?
Your child learns from you. When he sees your interest in books and enjoyment in reading, he picks up on your attitude and learns that reading is important – and fun!

I HEAR WORDS!

Phonological awareness

Being able to hear the smaller sounds in words helps children sound out written words

★ Phonological awareness involves hearing the similarities and differences between the sounds that make up words. Being able to identify and create rhymes is part of this important skill.

★ Talking and singing with your child, sharing finger plays, and reading books with rhymes all help prepare your child to sound out words as she learns to read.

★ This chapter offers some ideas and activities to help your child hear the smaller sounds in words.

Nonsense words

Even silly-sounding nonsense words and rhymes like "hickory dickory," "oopsey-doopsey," and "okey-dokey" are helpful in developing phonological awareness. Play at making up your own silly words and rhymes.

HICKORY DICKORY DOCK

Hickory dickory dock,	*(Bend arm up at elbow)*
The mouse ran up the clock,	*(Run fingers up arm)*
The clock struck one,	*(Clap loudly once)*
The mouse ran down,	*(Run fingers back down arm)*
Hickory dickory dock.	

The clock struck two, the mouse said, "BOO!"
The clock struck three, the mouse said, "WHEE!"
The clock struck four, the mouse said, "NO MORE!"

"Hickory Dickory Dock" is a rhyme that can be easily adapted. For younger children, you might use just the first verse as a simple bounce. Older children can sway back and forth to the words "Hickory dickory dock" and really act it out.

✔ TIP

Be sure to give a baby's head extra support during bounces until she is strong enough to hold her head steady herself.

Developmental milestones

Children learn at different rates. You may observe the following behaviours related to phonological awareness skills in your child.

Babies:
★ Can copy sounds and actions you make
★ Start recognizing words
★ Use sounds to get attention

Toddlers:
★ Can repeat a familiar rhyme
★ Can combine words into simple sentences

Preschoolers:
★ Show familiarity with rhyming and beginning sounds
★ Participate in rhyming games.

DID YOU KNOW?
Most children who have difficulty reading have trouble hearing the smaller sounds in words.

❄ *Out Came the Sun:*
A Day in Nursery Rhymes
♣ Heather Collins, 2007
This adorable collection of nursery rhymes follows an animal family through their fun-filled day.

❄ *Sing a Song of Mother Goose*
♣ Barbara Reid, 2008
As one of Canada's leading author/ illustrators, Barbara Reid's amazing artwork brings to life favourite traditional rhymes.

Rhymes and nursery rhyme books

Rhyming helps your child understand that words are made of smaller parts.

★ Nursery rhymes are usually short and easy to remember. They make ideal portable "playthings" for you and your child.

★ Sing, read or say rhymes at any time – at bath or change time, while eating or before bed. Anytime, any place!

★ Many collections of nursery rhymes, or Mother Goose rhymes, can be found in your library.

★ When choosing nursery rhyme books, a one-rhyme book is ideal for babies, while one rhyme per page works well for toddlers. Preschoolers are ready for more rhymes.

★ Make up words that rhyme with your child's name.

Play with nursery rhymes

★ Read or sing a nursery rhyme and ask your child to listen for the rhyme. For example, try reciting "Hickory, dickory, dock. The mouse ran up the clock!" and point out the rhyming words "dock" and "clock." Then try a different rhyme and ask your child to find the rhyming words.

★ As a variation, say most of the rhyme, but leave out the rhyming last word and ask your child to provide it. For example, "Jack and Jill went up the _____" (hill). Or try "Up above the world so high, like a diamond in the _____" (sky).

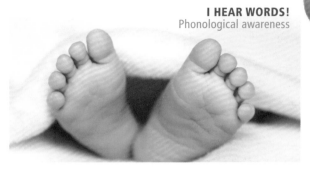

Children and poetry

Sharing nursery rhymes and poetry is one of the best ways to introduce your child to rhyming words.

★ For very young babies, try rhymes that involve a gentle touch, such as patting their feet.

★ Play with your child by making up short rhymes and poems together.

Hearing sounds

Being able to hear and recognize the beginning, middle and ending sounds that make up words helps children sound out words when they begin to read.

FROM WIBBLETON TO WOBBLETON

Face your child toward you to see each other's expressions and enjoy bonding. Bounce your child on your knee in time to the rhythm. It's fun to bounce "Wibbleton" toward one side, and "Wobbleton" to the other side. "15 miles" is somewhere in the middle.

From Wibbleton to Wobbleton is 15 miles.
From Wobbleton to Wibbleton is 15 miles.
From Wibbleton to Wobbleton,
From Wobbleton to Wibbleton,
From Wobbleton to Wibbleton is 15 miles.

LEG OVER LEG

This rhyme is good to use while changing a baby's diaper. It can also be used as a bouncing rhyme with your toddler, or acted out by your three to five year old.

With baby on table, hold ankles and cross legs; lift legs on last line.

Leg over leg, the dog went to Dover.
When he came to a fence –
Jump! He went over.

No Matter What
Emma Dodd, 2007
Mama elephant will always love her baby… no matter what. This book told in rhyme will appeal to both babies and toddlers.

Alligator Pie
♣ Dennis Lee, 1974
Illus. Frank Newfeld
This poetry book is a true classic of Canadian children's literature.

DID YOU KNOW?
Repetition strengthens connections in your child's developing brain. Repeat rhymes and songs so your child can become familiar with them and really master them.

Listening and rhythm

When you march, dance or sing together, you break up words into smaller sounds.

★ Add actions as you sing a song or recite a poem. Actions help children break down language into separate words.

★ Add clapping, tapping, drumming, bouncing, walking, marching, jumping and dancing activities to language. For example, clap your baby's hands or have your toddler clap along to the rhyme, music or song.

★ Say a word to your child and ask him to count the number of sounds he hears, and show the number by holding up his fingers, jumping up and down, or clapping. For example, "porcupine" has three sounds or syllables – "por-cu-pine." Your child would jump three times.

> **DID YOU KNOW?**
> Playing fun listening games like "Simon Says" is good for improving your child's listening skills.

Rhythm instruments

If you don't have a rattle to shake to the rhythm of the music or song, you can make one. Seal beans, uncooked rice, cereal or popcorn in a small unbreakable container to use as a shaker or maraca. Play with your child and say "shake, shake" each time your child shakes the container.

Rhyme & rhythm

This rhyme is great to clap along to. See if your child will copy your actions. With older children, try clapping your hands against their hands. In place of clapping, you can tap your knees or stamp your feet to the rhythm. Rub your tummy, smile and say "yummy, yummy" at the end.

PEASE PORRIDGE HOT

Pease porridge hot.
Pease porridge cold.
Pease porridge in the pot,
Nine days old.
Some like it hot.
Some like it cold.
Some like it in the pot,
Nine days old.

Sing!

Singing songs is an excellent way to help children hear the smaller, different sounds in words because each syllable in a word often gets its own musical note.

★ Don't worry about how you sound – from birth, your child loves to hear your voice.

★ Sing songs or rhymes in the language that is most comfortable for you. Young children don't need to understand the words for these moments together to be learning experiences.

★ Songs and music also help your child learn rhythm.

★ Suggestions for music CDs are listed on page 64.

This Little Chick
John Lawrence, 2002
Play with all the different animal noises as the little chick walks around the barnyard. Ask your child to make the animal sounds.

✳ **On My Walk**
♣ Kari-Lynn Winters, 2009
Illus. Christina Leist
Listen to the sounds heard on a summer walk, as a child and mother get caught in the rain and run back home.

Toot Toot Beep Beep
Emma Garcia, 2008
Kids will have fun making the sounds of the many colourful cars on this trip until they're all quiet in the parking lot.

Whispering games

Practise listening skills. Whisper from different parts of the room and ask your child where the sound is coming from.

DID YOU KNOW?
While you read together, your child may not seem to be paying attention, but she may surprise you with what she has learned.

Throughout the day

Add songs, rhyming and language games to your activities throughout the day.

★ Books that celebrate sounds and noises all around give young children practice in listening.

★ Books of simple, familiar songs are good choices for young listeners.

Dial-a-Story
416-395-5400

Listen to your favourite stories over the phone in many different languages.

torontopubliclibrary.ca/dial-a-story

DID YOU KNOW?
Playing with words like cat/hat/bat in songs and rhymes builds phonological awareness — the ability to hear the smaller sounds in words.

Eat your words

Using crackers, cereal, or another food, say a word and ask your child to eat the same number of items as the sounds in the word. For example, "bookmark" has two sounds, so your child would eat two crackers.

Try tongue twisters

Tongue twisters are useful for encouraging children to hear the similar sound at the beginning of many words. Books with alliteration are also fun.

PETER PIPER

Peter Piper picked a peck of pickled peppers.
A peck of pickled peppers Peter Piper picked.
If Peter Piper picked a peck of pickled peppers,
Where's the peck of pickled peppers Peter Piper picked?

Song writing

Make up your own words and verses to familiar songs throughout the day and have fun acting them out.

RING AROUND THE ROSIE

Ring around the rosie, a pocketful of posies,
(Children hold hands and go around in a circle)

A-husha! A-husha! We all fall down!
(Everybody sits on the floor)

Picking up the daisies, picking up the daisies,
(Children pretend to pick flowers)

A-husha! A-husha! We all stand up!
(Everybody jumps up)

Animal sound match

Play at matching an animal with the sound one makes. When children can imitate animal noises they are also learning to hear the sounds in words, developing the skill that helps them sound out words when learning to read.

OLD MACDONALD HAD A FARM

Old MacDonald had a farm, E-I-E-I-O.

And on his farm he had a cow, E-I-E-I-O.

With a moo, moo here and a moo, moo there,

Here a moo, there a moo,

Everywhere a moo-moo.

Old MacDonald had a farm, E-I-E-I-O.

You can continue adding as many animals as you like, replacing the cow, but following the pattern.

For example:

…And on his farm he had a pig, E-I-E-I-O.
With an oink, oink here and an oink, oink there…

YOUR TURN!

Answer these together

Who sings songs with me?

My favourite song is:

My favourite rhyme is:

My favourite bounce is:

My favourite funny word is:

I like to clap along to:

I like to jump to:

What words rhyme with "cat?"

Bee-bim Bop!
Linda Sue Park, 2005
Illus. Ho Baek Lee
A little girl helps her mother shop for and prepare a favourite meal of delicious Bee-bim Bop.

Llama Llama Red Pajama
Anna Dewdney, 2005
After being tucked into bed by his mother, baby llama doesn't want to be left alone. This reassuring tale is told in rhyme.

I KNOW WORDS!

Vocabulary

Knowing many words helps children recognize written words and understand what they read

★ Vocabulary is about knowing the names of things, feelings, ideas and concepts (like more or less, and before or after).

★ Hearing and understanding many words helps children sound them out when they are learning to read.

★ This chapter offers some ideas and activities to help your child learn more words.

New words

Rhymes and books help teach many new words that children may not hear in everyday conversation.

TEN LITTLE FINGERS

I have ten little fingers,	*(Hold up all ten fingers)*
And they all belong to me.	*(Point to self)*
I can make them do things,	
Would you like to see?	
I can shut them up tight;	*(Make fists)*
I can open them wide;	*(Extend fingers)*
I can put them together;	*(Clasp hands)*
And I can make them all hide.	*(Hide hands behind back)*
I can put them up high;	*(Reach hands above head)*
I can put them down low;	*(Touch floor with hands)*
I can fold them together,	*(Clasp hands and intertwine fingers)*
And hold them just so.	*(Place hands in lap)*

WHAT ARE THESE FOR?

Hold up both hands asking "What are these for? Hands are for folding." Fold your hands together. "And hands are for clapping!" Clap hands together.

Encourage your child to copy your words and actions.

Continue with other body parts:
Toes – tapping, tickling, etc.
Eyes – sleeping, looking, etc.
Nose – sniffing, sneezing, etc.

Developmental milestones

Vocabulary begins to develop at birth and continues to grow throughout life. Here are some common stages in building vocabulary.

Babies:

★ Can understand the names of some familiar people and objects

★ Babble and try to "talk" with you

Toddlers:

★ Can verbalize desires and feelings

★ Are familiar with the main parts of the body

Preschoolers:

★ Know the names of familiar animals

★ Can name common objects in picture books

★ Can create longer sentences.

DID YOU KNOW?
Children develop larger vocabularies the more time they spend talking and reading with family members.

Babies talk

Start talking to your baby in your home language on the day he is born.

★ By babbling, babies learn to make sounds with their own voices. Encourage your baby to become more vocal by responding to his coos, gurgles and grunts to promote language development.

★ When your child says "Aaah," say it back to her, and turn the sounds into real words. Encourage your child to copy you, too. You'll help your child recognize which sounds form language, and develop her vocabulary before she can talk.

• When your child babbles or talks, listen carefully and answer. Even if you don't know what he means or he doesn't have the words to answer, talk to your child and ask him lots of questions.

Nursery rhymes

Rhymes are an excellent way to build vocabulary.

I'M A LITTLE TEAPOT

I'm a little teapot, short and stout.
Here is my handle, and here is my spout.
(Right hand is on hip, left arm is bent at the elbow with hand pointing to the side)
When I get all steamed up, hear me shout.
Just tip me over and pour me out.

Ten Tiny Tickles
Karen Katz, 2005
Greet baby's day with tickles!

Eyes, Nose, Fingers, and Toes: A First Book All About You
Judy Hindley, 1999
Illus. Brita Granström
It's fun to learn the names of all the parts of your body.

Where is the Green Sheep?
Mem Fox, 2004
Illus. Judy Horacek
Our green sheep must be here, somewhere… Let's look!

When Sophie Gets Angry – Really, Really Angry…
Molly Bang, 1999
Everyone feels angry sometimes.

Parts of the body

Some of the first words babies learn are for different parts of their bodies. Rhymes and songs are a fun way to learn, in any language.

HEAD AND SHOULDERS

Sing to the tune of "London Bridge is Falling Down." Have your child copy you and touch each body part.

Head and shoulders,
Knees and toes, knees and toes, knees and toes.
Head and shoulders, knees and toes,
Eyes, ears, mouth and nose.

You can sing this with your baby, gently touching the parts of the body. Toddlers and preschoolers enjoy this rhyme as an action song. This rhyme is fun to perform faster and faster and faster.

HANA, HANA, HANA A Japanese face poem

Touch the body part as you say the word for it.

Hana, hana, hana.   *(Touch nose)*
Kutchi, kutchi, kutchi.   *(Touch mouth)*
Mimi, mimi, mimi.   *(Touch ears)*
Mei.   *(Point to eyes)*

ONLINE VIDEO

Visit **torontopubliclibrary.ca/ readyforreading** to view a video performance of fun rhymes like this one.

Play with music

Sing throughout the day and make up your own silly songs to introduce new vocabulary.

★ New words can be easier to learn when they rhyme or are put to music.

★ Many activities can be sung to the tune of "Here We Go 'Round the Mulberry Bush." For example, in the bathtub, wash your child while singing "This is the way I wash my face…" adding your own verses.

★ Let your child help make up new words to familiar songs.

DID YOU KNOW?
Books offer richer vocabulary than ordinary daily conversation. Your child hears more new words when you read books with her every day.

Use new words

Practise saying new words together.

★ Take the time to stop and explain unfamiliar words when reading or speaking with your child.

★ Speak clearly when introducing new words.

★ When a word has more than one meaning, talk about the different meanings.

★ When talking with your child, use a variety of descriptive words.

★ Use specific words instead of words like "it," "here" or "there."

★ For familiar words in a book, rhyme or song, think of a new word that has a similar meaning.

★ When a child is learning a new word, use it often throughout the day. Be patient as you re-read the same story over and over.

DID YOU KNOW?
Repeating new words is important. Repetition helps your child's brain link sound and meaning.

The Very Hungry Caterpillar
Eric Carle, 1987
A very hungry caterpillar eats its way through the pages of this wholly irresistible book.

Fancy Nancy
Jane O'Connor, 2006
Illus. Robin Preiss Glasser
Why be plain when you can be fancy? Vocabulary is "fancy" for words.

❋ ***One Watermelon Seed***
♣ Celia Barker Lottridge, 2008
Illus. Karen Patkau
Count the seeds to plant and their bountiful crops in Max and Josephine's garden.

Dim Sum for Everyone!
Grace Lin, 2001
At a dim sum restaurant, a family picks their favourite dishes from steaming trolleys.

What's for lunch?

You'll discover all sorts of new words when you cook with your child. What fantastic meals can your child invent for you? New experiences usually introduce new vocabulary.

I HAD A LITTLE TURTLE

I had a little turtle,	*(Make a fist with thumb sticking out)*
He lived in a box.	*(Cup hands together for a box)*
He swam in a puddle.	*(Wiggle hand for swimming)*
He climbed on the rocks.	*(Fingers climb up other fist)*
He snapped at a mosquito,	*(Snap fingers)*
He snapped at a flea,	*(Snap)*
He snapped at a minnow,	*(Snap)*
And he snapped at me!	*(Snap)*
He caught the mosquito,	*(Clap, gulp)*
He caught the flea,	*(Clap, gulp)*
He caught the minnow,	*(Clap, gulp)*
But he didn't catch me!	*(Wag pointer finger back and forth)*

ROW, ROW, ROW YOUR BOAT

Support your baby against your chest and rock back and forth in rhythm; sit older child facing you, hold her hands, and rock back and forth.

Row, row, row your boat
Gently down the stream.
Merrily, merrily, merrily, merrily,
Life is but a dream.

Row, row, row your boat down the jungle stream,
If you see a crocodile, don't forget to scream!

ONLINE VIDEO

Visit **torontopubliclibrary.ca/readyforreading** to view a video performance of fun rhymes like this one.

While reading

Children learn best by doing – and they love doing things with YOU.

★ While sharing books with your child, encourage her to talk about the story and pictures, instead of just listening to you read.

★ Invite him to participate by asking questions. Ask, "What's that?" and point to and name pictures in a book.

★ Ask questions like, "Where is the dog?" or, "What is the doggy doing?" Then add more describing words to what your child says, including the character's feelings, even if those words are not used in the book.

★ Focus on a few new words in each book you read together. Practise saying them together and repeat them in other situations.

Dinosaur Roar!
Paul and Henrietta Stickland, 1994
This rhyming book of opposites introduces all sorts of dinosaurs as they head for lunch.

Big, Bigger, Biggest!
Nancy Coffelt, 2009
After reading this colourful book, your vocabulary will be jumbo, gigantic, colossal!

Talking is important

The more you talk with your child, the richer your child's vocabulary will be.

* Talk about and explain what you're doing and what's going on around you.

* Point at and name items as you see them.

* Whether you're bathing your child or taking a walk, use words that describe the actions and the things around you. Talk about all the senses involved.

* Help your child learn new words for concepts and ideas, as well as objects. More/less and before/after are examples of concepts.

* Talk about feelings – yours and your child's. Having the words to express feelings may help reduce your child's frustration.

DID YOU KNOW?
Most two year olds can understand 300 to 500 words, and most children enter school knowing between 3,000 to 5,000 words.

Play games

You are your child's first and favourite playmate.

MY TURN, YOUR TURN

Face your child. Touch your tummy and say, "Look! Here is daddy's tummy!" Ask your child, "Do you have a tummy? Where is your tummy?"

Help your child find her tummy. Now, point to her tummy and ask (as if you've forgotten), "What's this again?" This gives your child a chance to name the body part herself. Continue in this way with other body parts.

BRAINSTORMING GAMES

Think of a category such as animals, foods, round things, red things or things that grow. Take turns with your child thinking of different words that fit into that category.

I SPY GAME

Say, "I spy with my little eye, something that is …" and ask your child to find something according to a category, like shape, colour or size.

YOUR TURN!

Answer these together

My first word:

My favourite words:

People I know:

Games I play:

Food I eat:

Clothes I wear:

Places I go:

Songs I sing:

Naming, labelling and sorting

Once your child starts talking, help him find the words for things around him. Make a game of labelling items in your home together. When you are running errands, point out things in the neighbourhood and in the shops.

COLLAGE COLLECTION

Make a collection of magazine pictures that are alike in some way. If your child loves pets, collect pictures of dogs, cats, fish and birds. Label each picture clearly.

SORT YOUR SETS

Find four magazine pictures in the same category and paste each picture on a card. Make five sets of category cards and then mix them up. Ask your child to sort them.

MATCH ME UP

Collect pictures of things your child can easily find in your house: fruits, toys, furniture or household objects. Show your child a picture. Say, "Oh look! Here is a picture of an apple. I know there is a real apple around here somewhere. Can you find it?" Have your child bring you the object and compare it to the picture.

I CAN TELL A STORY!

Narrative skills

Learning to tell a story helps children develop skills in thinking and understanding

★ Narrative skills include the ability to describe things; to tell events in order; to tell and retell stories.

★ Understanding how stories work, that stories have a beginning, a middle and an end, is key to reading comprehension.

★ This chapter offers some ideas and activities to help your child develop narrative skills and reading comprehension.

What are narratives?

Narratives are stories with a beginning, a middle and an end, like these familiar nursery rhymes.

HUMPTY DUMPTY

"Humpty Dumpty" can be chanted, clapped or bounced, swooping child downward for the "great fall."

Humpty Dumpty sat on a wall.
Humpty Dumpty had a great fall.
All the king's horses,
And all the king's men,
Couldn't put Humpty together again.

THE EENSY, WEENSY SPIDER

To make a spider, place your right thumb on left forefinger, left thumb on right forefinger. Swivel fingers upward in a walking motion.

The eensy, weensy spider
Climbed up the water spout.   *(Crawl fingers upward)*
Down came the rain   *(Wiggle fingers down)*
And washed the spider out.   *(Brush hands to side)*
Out came the sun   *(Circle arms above head)*
And dried up all the rain.
And the eensy, weensy spider   *(Crawl fingers up again)*
Climbed up the spout again.

▶ ONLINE VIDEO

Visit **torontopubliclibrary.ca/readyforreading** to view a video performance of fun rhymes like this one.

Developmental milestones

What comes next? Daily routines, including sharing books, help children learn about the narrative structure of beginning, middle and end.

Babies:

★ May recognize and start to laugh at the first few words of a familiar rhyme

★ Anticipate elements of a repeated nursery rhyme such as a tickle

★ Enjoy playing peek-a-boo games

Toddlers:

★ May enjoy looking at one book over and over

★ Recall events of the day

★ May "read" to stuffed animals or toys

Preschoolers:

★ May like to play dress-up

★ Can follow directions with three or more steps

★ May make predictions based on the pictures in a storybook.

DID YOU KNOW?

Children with good narrative skills are better able to understand what they read.

As you read together...

Take some time to talk together about the book. It's easy to do.

★ You don't have to read a book from cover to cover without stopping. Point to the pictures and ask questions like, "What's this?" or, "What is he doing?" Give your child time to answer, and then praise her efforts. Encourage your child to ask questions, too.

★ Add to what your child says. If your child says, "Big truck," you might say, "That's right! The firefighter is driving a big, red fire truck!"

★ Help your child understand the story. Ask questions such as, "Why do you think the little girl was happy?" or, "What do you think is happening in this picture?" Try to ask questions that can't be answered with "yes" or "no."

★ As you talk together, your child practises his language skills. Sharing a book in this way is called "dialogic reading."

Play

Children learn about their world through play. Play gives them the opportunity to learn and practise new skills.

PLAY MAKE BELIEVE

Encourage play by supplying dress-up clothes and props such as hats, scarves, backpacks, bowls and containers. As children act out their story, they are developing narrative skills.

SILLY SOUP

Make pretend soup. You will need a saucepan with a lid, a spoon and some small objects. Say, "Let's make soup!" and ask, "What do you think we should have in our soup?" Let your child choose an object, tell you what it is and place it in the saucepan. Then it's your turn. Say, "I think we should put some socks in the soup!" When there are three ingredients in the soup, ask your child to stir it and put on the lid. Scratch your head and ask, "Now, what is in our soup? Can you remember what delicious things are in it?" See if your child can recall the ingredients.

TELEPHONE TALK

Give your child a toy telephone, or a real phone that isn't in service. Make the phone "ring" and say "Oh! Your telephone is ringing! It must be your friend _____." Then talk to your child on your own telephone. Pretend to be the friend calling, ask your child about her day, and then finish by suggesting that you talk again tomorrow. The next day, play the game again.

※*Grumpy Bird*
🍁 Jeremy Tankard, 2007
Even though Bird wakes up so grumpy he doesn't want to fly, his friends stick with him until he feels better.

Lola at the Library
Anna McQuinn, 2006
Illus. Rosalind Beardshaw
On Tuesdays, Lola goes to the library with her mother.

What's next?

Look at a book's front cover and ask your child what he thinks the story will be about.

★ Look at the pictures, and ask your child what he thinks will happen next. It's fun to read and compare the prediction with what really happens.

★ Wordless picture books are great for practising narrative skills. By giving children a chance to tell a story in their own words, they build their storytelling skills and are encouraged to use descriptive language.

✔ **TIP:** Search for "stories without words" on the library website.

Draw

Have your child draw a picture and tell you about it. Or, after reading a book, your child could draw a picture about something that happened in the story and tell you about that.

Design-a-Bookmark Contest

Winners receive a book prize and are featured on KidsSpace, Toronto Public Library's website for kids.

The contest is open to kids of all ages. Watch our website or ask at your local branch for an entry form.

torontopubliclibrary.ca/kidsspace

🍁 Canadian   ※ First & Best selection

Choosing books

Books especially good for developing narrative skills have stories that are fun to tell over and over again.

★ Let your child fill in a repeated part of a story, or complete a pattern. Encourage participation by saying a repeated line together.

★ Ask questions like "What happened first? And then? What happened in the end?"

★ Read and re-read your child's favourite books. Your child becomes more familiar with the story, building her understanding and making it easier for her to retell the story.

DID YOU KNOW?
Telling a story and solving math problems use similar skills.

Kitten's First Full Moon
Kevin Henkes, 2004
Poor Kitten, she just cannot reach that delectable-looking bowl of milk she sees high up in the sky.

Three Billy Goats Gruff
Paul Galdone, 2001
In this traditional tale, three goats want to visit the green pasture on the other side of the river, but a fearsome troll guards the bridge.

The Paper Bag Princess
♣ Robert Munsch, 1980
Illus. Michael Martchenko
When a dragon burns her clothes and captures her fiancé, Princess Elizabeth is forced to wear a paper bag and engage the dragon in a battle of wits.

We're Going on a Bear Hunt
Michael Rosen, 1989
Illus. Helen Oxenbury
Brave hunters must overcome many obstacles before they find the fierce bear in its cave.

THIS LITTLE PIGGY

Play on fingers or toes.

This little piggy went to market.
This little piggy stayed home.
This little piggy had roast beef.
This little piggy had none.
And this little piggy ran wee, wee, wee, all the way home.

A tickle is a tiny story building to a predictable climax. A rhyme like "This Little Piggy" allows the anticipation to build for the tickle at the end.

Material in your own language

Kids can explore books, music, DVDs and stories in more than 67 languages available in our collections.

torontopubliclibrary.ca/ yourlanguage

What happens first, next and last?

Encourage your child to tell you about his day, or something that happened like a birthday party or a special trip.

★ Ask questions like, "What happened first? What happened next? What did it look like? What did you like best?"

★ Ask your child to tell you about things he does that have a regular order to them, like taking a bath.

★ Reading at bedtime is ideal for spending quiet moments with your child. Sharing stories of what happened during the day is a great way to develop narrative skills. It is another opportunity to talk about a child's daily routines, which are stories themselves.

Puppet play

Ask your child to tell you a story using puppets. You can buy hand or finger puppets, or make them. For example, cut out pictures and glue them to popsicle sticks. Help your child retell or act out her favourite story. Using puppets, toys, dolls or other props to tell a story may help your child remember it.

HERE IS A BUNNY

This rhyme can be done as a finger play or you could use a rabbit puppet or doll if you have one.

Here is a bunny,	*(Hold up two bent fingers)*
With ears so funny.	*(Wiggle the fingers)*
Here is his hole in the ground.	*(Make circle with thumb and four fingers of other hand)*
When a noise he hears, he pricks up his ears,	*(Straighten two fingers in 'V' shape)*
And jumps in his hole in the ground.	*(Jump fingers into hole on other hand)*

Talk. Talk. Talk.

And talk some more.

★ Babies love to hear your voice. Copy your baby's sounds and listen to the sounds she makes back. Take the time throughout the day to talk with your child about all kinds of things. For example, talk to her about the weather. Ask older children to describe what it's like outside. Complete this sentence: Today the weather is_____.

★ Describe daily activities. Talk about what has happened, what is happening and what will happen during the day. Even with your baby, talk about what you are doing: "Now we're going to change your diaper, and then we are going to have a bottle, and after that we are going to have a nap."

★ Your child will listen to the way you describe what you're doing and how you structure your stories.

Bedtime game

At any time during the day, play the bedtime game. Together, put a favourite toy to bed. Make the bedtime routine as elaborate as you like. Play versions of this game where your child puts you or another family member to bed.

Describe with your senses

As you go about your day, use all your senses when you talk about what you are doing. For example, as you make dinner, you might say, "Look at all those yellow noodles I'm cooking! Can you hear the water bubbling in the pot? Take a deep breath and smell the red, tomato sauce. Mmmm… the sauce tastes very spicy!"

Goodnight Moon
Margaret Wise Brown, 1947
Illus. Clement Hurd
This classic book is perfect for bedtime. After sharing this story with your child, say goodnight to all the things in your child's bedroom.

The Napping House
Audrey Wood, 1984
Illus. Don Wood
On a rainy afternoon, everyone is asleep in the big cosy bed, except for one little flea.

Listen. Listen. Listen.

Make sure your child has lots of opportunities to talk with you.

★ Listen attentively as your child tries to tell you something. Even if you cannot understand what your child is saying, be a patient listener.

★ When your child tells a story, use plenty of praise and support.

★ Your child may "talk your ear off" and ask endless questions starting with, "Why." Encourage this curiosity and interest.

★ Together, look at a book that your child already knows. This time, let your child tell the story in his own way while you listen.

YOUR TURN!

Answer these together

Who tells me stories?

How do I get dressed?

How do I get ready for bedtime?

What is my favourite story about?

Let's make up a story:
Today we went to the library and …

❄ *A Visitor for Bear*
🍁 Bonny Becker, 2008
Illus. Kady MacDonald Denton
Bear likes living alone. Can a bright-eyed mouse make him change his mind?

On Mother's Lap
Ann Herbert Scott, 1992
Illus. Glo Coalson
There is always room for one more on Mother's lap in this gentle story set in the far north.

DID YOU KNOW?
Talking about their day helps children build storytelling skills. These skills help children understand what they read.

🍁 Canadian   ❄ First & Best selection

I SEE WORDS!

Print awareness

Being familiar with printed language helps children feel comfortable with books and reading

★ Print awareness includes noticing that print is all around and has meaning.

★ Before learning how to read a book, a child must learn what a book is, how words work and how letters represent words.

★ This chapter offers some ideas and activities to help your child become comfortable with printed language, books and reading.

THE WHEELS ON THE BUS

Have your child copy your actions.

The wheels on the bus go round and round,
(Trace circles with index fingers)
Round and round, round and round.
The wheels on the bus go round and round,
All through the town.

Repeat the song substituting:
The doors on the bus go open and shut…
(Bring hands apart then together)
The people on the bus go up and down…
(Bounce up and down)
The driver on the bus says, "Move on back!…"
(Point toward back)
The babies on the bus go, "Wah, wah, wah…"
(Open mouth and wipe eyes with fists, as if crying)
The parents on the bus say, "Shh, shh, shh…"
(Put finger to lips for "Shh" sounds)
The wipers on the bus go swish, swish, swish…
(Palms face out, move them side to side)
The horn on the bus goes honk, honk, honk…
(Pretend to honk horn) (Repeat first verse)

You can adapt this song to your own car trips. For example:
"The mommy in the car says, 'Buckle up! Buckle up! Buckle
up!'" Invite your children to add their own silly verses to
this song.

Developmental milestones

When books are available in the home, a child goes quickly from chewing a board book to enjoying both words and pictures.

Babies:

★ Look at books and point to pictures

★ Give books to adults to read to them

Toddlers:

★ Scribble on paper with a purpose and tell you what they wrote or drew

★ Begin to pay attention to specific print such as the first letters of their names

★ Turn books right side up; can turn pages with your help

Preschoolers:

★ Identify familiar signs and labels

★ Have an understanding of the function of print

★ Know that print has a message.

Pointing to words

Pointing to words as you read them helps your child become familiar with printed language.

★ As you run your finger underneath the words, you show that the printed word and the story are connected.

★ Books with large print or with few words on a page are especially good for pointing.

★ Point to a word that interests your child and words that are repeated as you read them.

★ Run your child's finger underneath the words as you read or, using a book that your child knows well, ask him to point to the words as you read them.

★ These activities help your child see that, in English, we read from the top of the page to the bottom, from left to right, and that written words have a space between them. Your child is also learning that it's the print on the page being read, and not the pictures.

DID YOU KNOW?
Most books, rhymes, songs and activities develop more than one skill.

Where should I start?

Before reading a story, introduce the cover and title, and talk about the author and illustrator.

Say things like, "Let's start at the beginning" and "Let's read the words."

First words

Up, down, in, out, fast and slow are some of the first words in print that your child may start to recognize.

ROLY POLY, ROLY POLY

Roll hands around each other.

Roly poly, roly poly,
Up, up, up. Up, up, up.
Roly, roly, poly. Roly, roly, poly,
Down, down, down. Down, down, down.
Roly poly, roly poly,
Out, out, out. Out, out, out.
Roly, roly, poly. Roly, roly, poly,
In, in, in. In, in, in.
Roly poly, roly poly,
Fast, fast, fast. Fast, fast, fast.
Roly, roly, poly. Roly, roly, poly,
Slow, slow, slow. Slow, slow, slow.

ONLINE VIDEO
Visit **torontopubliclibrary.ca/readyforreading** to view a video performance of fun rhymes like this one.

To Market, To Market
Anne Miranda, 1997
Illus. Janet Stevens
This lady has a very strange
shopping list that starts with a pig.

Clip-Clop
Nicola Smee, 2006
Mr. Horse is offering all of his barnyard
friends a ride on his back. All is well
until they fall off.

Read books

Read books with your child often.

★ Any book with words helps develop print awareness because
your child learns to recognize print, how books work and
how we use them.

★ Let your child hold the book and turn the pages of the book
as she "reads" to you or as you read together. Board books
are good for babies to practise turning pages.

★ Show your child that print is useful and that reading is
important to you by talking to him about what you are
reading: the newspaper, a book, a menu, a letter or an email.

Bouncing rhymes

These are good rhymes for a bounce or a gallop. Watch your child's face for clues to what she likes.

TO MARKET, TO MARKET

To market, to market, to buy a fat pig;
Home again, home again, jiggety jig.
To market, to market, to buy a fat hog;
Home again, home again, jiggety jog.
To market, to market, to buy a white cake;
Home again, home again, never was baked.
To market, to market, to buy a plum bun;
Home again, home again, market is done.
(Give your child a hug.)

BUMPIN' UP AND DOWN

Bumpin' up and down in my little red wagon.
Bumpin' up and down in my little red wagon.
Bumpin' up and down in my little red wagon.
Won't you be my darlin'!
One wheel's off and the axle's broken…
Freddie's gonna fix it with his hammer…
Laura's gonna fix it with her pliers…
Bumpin' up and down in my little red wagon.

✔ TIP

Be sure to give a
baby's head extra
support during
bounces until he is
strong enough to
hold his head steady
himself.

Print is all around

Even as a baby, your child will start to learn that printed words have meaning. Use every opportunity to read aloud.

* While walking or driving, point to and talk about street signs, traffic signs and billboards. Praise your child when she recognizes words like "Stop" on stop signs or "Open" in shop windows.

* Point out labels while shopping. Point to and read print on toys, T-shirts, posters and mugs.

* Other everyday print to read aloud might include lists, notes, letters, emails, menus, recipes, cereal boxes, directions, schedules, calendars and birthday cards.

DID YOU KNOW?
Children who recognize that reading is valuable will be motivated to learn how to read.

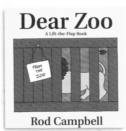

Dear Zoo
Rod Campbell, 2007
If you wrote to the zoo asking for a pet, what would they send you?

The Baby Goes Beep
Rebecca O'Connell, 2003
Illus. Ken Wilson-Max
Parents will relate to this energetic baby as he makes his way through the day.

Peekaboo Morning
Rachel Isadora, 2002
Who will the next peekaboo be…a bunny, a friend, grandma?

City Signs
Zoran Milich, 2002
Look at all the words that you can see as you go through the city!

Big Fat Hen
Keith Baker, 1994
In this book, a good choice for print awareness, there are only a few words per page.

Click Clack Moo: Cows that Type
Doreen Cronin, 2000
Illus. Betsy Lewin
When the cows find a typewriter in the barn, Farmer Brown's problems begin.

Signs, posters and traffic lights

Show your child the street names. Does your child know where he lives?

TRAFFIC LIGHTS
Green means go,
Yellow means slow,
And red means STOP!

DO YOU KNOW THE MUFFIN MAN

Do you know the muffin man,
The muffin man, the muffin man?
Do you know the muffin man,
Who lives in Drury Lane?
Yes, I know the muffin man,
The muffin man, the muffin man.
Yes, I know the muffin man,
Who lives in Drury Lane.

HOW MUCH IS THAT DOGGIE IN THE WINDOW?

How much is that doggie in the window?
The one with the waggly tail.
How much is that doggie in the window?
I do hope that doggie's for sale.

Scribble, write and draw

Encourage scribbling, writing and drawing in daily activities.

★ Give your child opportunities to practise "writing" her name or let her "write" notes or lists. Encourage her to draw as well.

★ Your child can draw a picture of what is happening in the book, or "write" words of a story.

★ Share your own writing. For example, a shopping list is one way to show your child that printed words represent real things.

★ Show your child how you write your shopping list (and let him "write" one too). At the store, read the list with your child and find the items together.

I love bookmobile

"Traffic Lights" lyrics reprinted by permission of Wendy Fine Music.

2006 Design-a-Bookmark Contest, Elizabeth Cleaver Award winner: Jessica Wu.

Language-rich environments

Print and books should be familiar and everyday items in your child's environment.

★ Allow your child to explore books by keeping a variety of books within reach.

★ Keep some books in your child's toy box.

★ Start a little library for your child keeping books on lower shelves.

★ Get into the habit of carrying a small picture book with you all the time.

★ Make a cosy nook just for reading together or alone.

★ Show your child how you make lists or write notes.

★ Make paper, pencils, markers, crayons, chalk and finger paints available for scribbling, writing and drawing.

★ Visit the public library often and regularly for a fun outing. Get your child her own library card.

Drumheller Dinosaur Dance
♣ Robert Heidbreder, 2004
Illus. Bill Slavin, Esperança Melo
By daylight, the Drumheller dinosaurs rest their ancient bones. But when the moon rises, so do these slumbering skeletons.

No, David!
David Shannon, 1998
The large print in this book makes it very clear what David should not do.

❉ *Roslyn Rutabaga and the Biggest Hole on Earth*
♣ Marie-Louise Gay, 2010
Roslyn Rutabaga has a plan – she is going to dig the biggest hole on Earth!

Play alien encounter

Pretend that you're from outer space and have never read a book before. Turn the book upside down, read it right to left, or mix the words up and allow your child to correct you. When the book is right side up, explain that it's so you can read it and start at the beginning. Use the words "front" and "back" of the book.

Play reporter

Let your child dictate to you as you write down his story, letter or list. Read it back together and then switch roles.

Background and general knowledge

Background knowledge helps children understand what they are reading.

★ Books, songs and rhymes introduce new ideas that build your child's understanding of the world.

★ Books often expose children to experiences outside their familiar environments and have pictures of things they may not see often.

★ Gain knowledge together by reading books on many different topics.

★ Non-fiction or information books use different words than those used in stories.

★ Exposing your child to new information, science and math concepts improves her reading comprehension.

★ Play offers opportunities to practise new vocabulary and builds knowledge.

Sophie's Studio

Sophie's Studio encourages children to discover their creativity and writing skills.

Children explore playing with writing at KidsStop Interactive Early Literacy Centres at various branches across the city. Find out more on our website:

torontopubliclibrary.ca/sophiesstudio

YOUR TURN!

Answer these together

What do people read at my house?

Who do I know who reads a newspaper?

What signs do I see on the street?

What would I like to eat? Make a menu.

What do we buy at the store? Make a list.

Let's plan a party. Who should we invite? Make a list.

I KNOW LETTERS!

Letter knowledge

Knowing the names and sounds of letters helps children to sound out words

★ Learning about different shapes is a child's first step to learning the letters of the alphabet.

★ To read, children must understand that written words are made of individual letters.

★ Knowing the different sounds of letters helps children figure out how to say written words.

★ This chapter offers some ideas and activities to help your child learn the names and sounds of letters.

The alphabet song

A perfect song for teaching letter knowledge – anytime, anywhere!

THE ALPHABET SONG, OR **THE ABC SONG**

Sing to the tune of "Twinkle, Twinkle Little Star."

A, B, C, D, E, F, G,

H, I, J, K, L, M, N, O, P,

Q, R, S, T, U, V,

W, X, Y and Z

Now I know my A, B, Cs,

Next time won't you sing with me?

Display an alphabet in your home and while you sing "The Alphabet Song," point to each letter or let your child do the pointing. This helps your child connect the name of the letter heard with the look of the letter.

Even if your child can sing "The Alphabet Song," she may still not have learned all the letters. It takes time to learn the look and sound of each letter.

Many different alphabet songs are available on CD to borrow from your local library.

 ONLINE VIDEO
Visit **torontopubliclibrary.ca/readyforreading** to view a video performance of an alphabet song and other fun rhymes.

Developmental milestones

A child needs to know the alphabet in order to read. Each child will learn at her own pace, but by age six almost all children will know all the letters and their sounds.

Babies:

★ Explore shapes by touching and mouthing

★ Learn to recognize and respond to their own names

Toddlers:

★ Can match simple shapes with each other

★ Start to use imaginary objects in play

Preschoolers:

★ Start to match letters with sounds

★ Recognize some letters, like the ones in their names.

DID YOU KNOW?
Young children can hear the sound of a letter most easily when it is at the beginning of a word.

Your child's name

Talk about the letters that are most interesting to your child – the letters in his name.

★ Help your child learn and recognize the first letter of her name. Together, look for that letter in a book. Eventually, your child will recognize and find all the letters of her name.

★ Say the names of the letters as you print your child's name.

★ Help your child write and read his own name.

★ Print your child's name on labels for her toys or other personal items.

Useful play

Rhymes and songs can be useful playthings that help guide your child's actions. This funny, little rhyme can ease children from a standing to a sitting position while building letter knowledge.

"A" IS FOR ALLIGATOR

"A" is for alligator, chomp, chomp, chomp.

"B" is for bouncing, up and down.

"C" is for circles, round and round.

"D" is for when we all sit down.

Round is a Mooncake
Roseanne Thong, 2000
Illus. Grace Lin
Picking out the shapes of objects in this book is an excellent beginning step to letter knowledge.

Mouse Shapes
Ellen Stoll Walsh, 2007
Look what three little mice can make with the shapes they find!

Chicka Chicka Boom Boom
Bill Martin, Jr. and John Archambault, 1989
Illus. Lois Ehlert
This classic features bold illustrations of letters falling from a coconut tree and a rhythmic chant.

ABC x 3
🍁 Marthe Jocelyn, 2005
Illus. Tom Slaughter
Simple illustrations and words in three languages introduce the letters of the alphabet to baby.

Interesting words

Help your child write and read words that interest him. Using magnetic letters, crayons, or pencil and paper, help him to write the names of family members, or words like "truck" or "book."

LETTER TILES

Use magnetic letters to create words with a pattern, such as "at." Change the first sound of the word by replacing the first letter with another. For example, change "cat" to "bat" by replacing the "c" with the "b."

RAINBOW NAME

Print your child's name on a piece of white paper. Ask your child to trace over the letters with different colours, until there is a rainbow around each letter of his name.

ME COLLAGE

Help your child look for the letters of her name in words on magazine pages. Cut out the letters and paste them down in order on paper. Now ask your child to look for words and pictures that tell about herself. Help to cut them out and paste them around her name.

Play with letters

Play games with alphabet blocks, felt or foam letters, or letters cut from newspapers or magazines. Try making simple words or your child's name.

★ Letters can also be made from string or cooked, cooled spaghetti. Your child may enjoy playing, writing and drawing in sand, pudding, sugar or flour.

★ First trace a letter on a page with your finger and then use your child's finger to trace the shape of the letter. Can your child trace the letter without your help?

★ Choose a "Letter of the Day" and point out everything you see, all day long, that starts with that letter.

★ Find and name letters in books, on signs and labels, on toys, food boxes and other objects all around.

★ Help your child roll modelling clay or playdough into thin "logs." Ask your child to use the logs to form the letters he is learning.

★ Play with magnetic letters on the refrigerator or on metal baking trays. Arrange the letters in alphabetical order. Remove a letter and ask your child which one is missing. Can she put the letter back into the correct space? Or, arrange the letters incorrectly and ask your child to put them into the correct order.

Shape games

Learning about different shapes, and recognizing them, helps your child learn how letters are formed and prepares him to learn the alphabet.

★ Help your child find shapes. What is round like a circle? A ball, a plate, a wheel? Can you find something shaped like a triangle? A slice of pizza? A piece of cheese?

★ Introduce your baby to shapes by running her hand along the length of a spoon or along the curves of a ball and talk about the shapes you are feeling.

★ Cut snacks into shapes. You could cut carrots or bananas into little circles or cut cheese into squares or triangles. Ask your child to identify the shapes.

★ Show your child items in different colours and shapes. As you pick up each thing, describe it. For example, "This is a ball. It's round and in the shape of a circle. Do you see the big, red ball?"

Rhymes with shapes

There are a number of rhymes, tickles and bounces that include shapes.

THE MOON IS ROUND

The moon is round, as round can be,
(Trace your finger around child's face)
Two eyes, a nose, and a mouth – like me!
(Point to body parts and end with a smile or a kiss)

ROUND AND ROUND THE GARDEN

Round and round the garden,
Goes the teddy bear.   *(Circle fingers around baby's tummy)*
One step. Two steps.   *(Walk fingers up chest)*
Tickle you under there!   *(Tickle baby under chin)*

A GREAT BIG BALL

A great big ball,
(Make a circle by joining hands over head)
A middle-sized ball,
(Make a circle by touching fingers and thumbs of both hands together)
A little ball I see.
(Make a circle with thumb and index finger)
Let's see if we can count them:
One, two, three.
(Repeat motions above)

CRISS CROSS APPLESAUCE

Criss Cross,   *(Draw X on baby's back)*
Applesauce,   *(Tap shoulders 3 times)*
Spiders climbing up your back.   *(Tickle baby's back)*
Cool breeze,   *(Blow on baby's neck)*
Tight squeeze,   *(Give baby a hug)*
Now you've got the shiveries!   *(Tickle all over)*

Play with puzzles

★ Simple puzzles help preschoolers see differences between shapes.

★ Help your child play with puzzles and encourage her to try a different space where the puzzle piece might fit.

★ You can make your own puzzles by taking a picture, backing it with a piece of construction paper, and cutting it into different shaped pieces.

★ Write your child's name on a strip of paper, leaving extra space between the letters. Cut apart the letters and mix them up. Ask your child to rearrange them in the order of her name. Play this game with other names or words of interest.

UPPER/lower case
The same letter can look different.

★ Show and teach your child that there is a big R and a little r; a big G and a little g.

★ With any book, not just an alphabet book, you can point out specific letters and talk about them.

★ Can your child find the same letter in upper case and lower case?

★ Choose two letters: How do they look alike? How do they look different? What shapes do they have in them?

Mystery trip

Ask your child to pretend she is packing a suitcase or backpack for a special trip, but only things that start with the same "special letter" can go in. For example, ask your child to pack items that begin with "f." Your child could pack flyers, a toy frog, and a frisbee. See how many items your child can find.

DID YOU KNOW?
Your child will develop Ready for Reading skills no matter what language you speak at home.

Mmmmm...

Sounds

Letter knowledge includes knowing that letters relate to sounds and that specific sounds go with specific letters.

★ When you talk about letters, say the name of the letter as well as the sound it makes.

★ Repeat letter sounds. "M" goes MMMMM. "B" goes BBBB.

★ Knowing the sounds of the letters helps children figure out how to say written words.

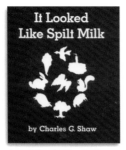

It Looked Like Spilt Milk
Charles G. Shaw, 1947
Fourteen white shapes on a deep blue background portray familiar and less familiar objects.

First the Egg
Laura Vaccaro Seeger, 2007
Starting with the lovely oval of an egg, cut-out pages draw attention to all kinds of different shapes.

Same or different

Talk with your child about what is the same and what is different in things around you, or in the picture books you share.

MATCH-UPS

★ Letting your child help you pair up socks from the laundry can help him to see the differences in shapes and patterns.

★ Print upper case letters and clip each one to a clothespin. Ask your child to hang the letters and clothespins on a string, in alphabetical order.

★ As a variation, search for fun letter-matching items to hang from each clothespin. For example, pin up a sock for "s," or a zipper for "z."

★ Another variation: Write each letter in lower case and ask your child to match them to the upper case letters on the clothesline.

LETTER TICKLERS

Tape a feather onto the end of a straw. After reading a page of a story, ask your child to "tickle" a letter. For example, ask your child to tickle all of the r's on a page from *Red is Best* by Kathy Stinson.

Books

Many books have print that is large and easy to read.

★ Read books that feature shapes.

★ Look at books where you have to find things (like *I Spy* books).

★ Read alphabet books that link the letter to an object such as: "A is for apple."

★ Alphabet books do not need to be read from A to Z. You can let your child choose what letters and pictures to talk about. Listen, and then talk about the letter and its sound.

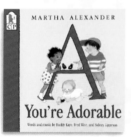

A You're Adorable
Buddy Kaye, Fred Wise and
Sidney Lippman, 1994
Illus. Martha Alexander
This old song is brought
to life with whimsical
illustrations of children.

***The Sleepy Little Alphabet: A
Bedtime Story from Alphabet Town***
Judy Sierra, 2009
Illus. Melissa Sweet
Alphabet letters get ready for bed.
Upper case letters are parents, and the
children are lower case.

Answer these together

A is for animals I like:

B is for books I like:

C is for colours I like:

F is for friends I like:

My name starts with the letter:

I can write my name:

DID YOU KNOW?
Helping your child learn the letters
of the alphabet is one sure way to
help him succeed
at school.

Our 2007–2012 top picks of the best Canadian children's books for building reading readiness in kids under five. Because the first books you share with your child should also be the best!

Along a Long Road
Frank Viva, 2011

Animal Masquerade
Marianne Dubuc, 2012

Baby's Lullaby
Jili Barber, 2010
Illus. HildaRose

Better Together
Sheryl and Simon Shapiro, 2011
Illus. Dušan Petričić

Boo Hoo Bird
Jeremy Tankard, 2009

Canada in Words
Per-Henrik Gürth, 2012

Caramba and Henry
Marie-Louise Gay, 2011

Chicken, Pig, Cow
Ruth Ohi, 2008

Chicken, Pig, Cow Horse Around
Ruth Ohi, 2010

Cinnamon Baby
Nicola Winstanley, 2011
Illus. Janice Nadeau

Cookiebot!: A Harry and Horsie Adventure
Katie Van Camp, 2011
Illus. Lincoln Agnew

Crocodiles Play!
Robert Heidbreder, 2008
Illus. Rae Maté

Eats
Marthe Jocelyn, 2007
Illus. Tom Slaughter

Extra Yarn
Mac Barnett, 2012
Illus. Jon Klassen

Farley Follows His Nose
Lynn Johnston and
Beth Cruikshank, 2009
Illus. Lynn Johnston

Goodnight, Sweet Pig
Linda Bailey, 2007
Illus. Josée Masse

Grumpy Bird
Jeremy Tankard, 2007

Hockey Opposites
Per-Henrik Gürth, 2010

How Do You Read to a Rabbit?
Andrea Wayne von Königslöw, 2010

I Can Do It Myself!
(and **Now I Am Big!**)
Stephen Krensky, 2012
Illus. Sara Gillingham
(boardbook set of 2)

I Like to Play
Marla Stewart Konrad, 2009

It's a Tiger!
David LaRochelle, 2012
Illus. Jeremy Tankard

It's Moving Day
Pamela Hickman, 2008
Illus. Geraldo Valério

Kiss, Tickle, Cuddle, Hug
Susan Musgrave, 2012

Kitten's Autumn / Kitten's Spring
Eugenie Fernandes, 2010

Lickety-Split
Robert Heidbreder, 2007
Illus. Dušan Petričić

Little Panda
Renata Liwska, 2008

Mother Goose
Groundwood Books, 2009

Mr. Zinger's Hat
Cary Fagan, 2012
Illus. Dušan Petričić

Noisy Poems for a Busy Day
Robert Heidbreder, 2012
Illus. Lori Joy Smith

Off We Go!
Beverley Abramson, 2006

On My Walk
Kari-Lynn Winters, 2009
Illus. Christina Leist

One Watermelon Seed
Celia Barker Lottridge, 2008
Illus. Karen Patkau

Ones and Twos
Marthe Jocelyn
and Nell Jocelyn, 2011

**Out Came the Sun:
A Day in Nursery Rhymes**
Heather Collins, 2007

**A Paddling of Ducks: Animals
in Groups from A to Z**
Marjorie Blain Parker, 2010
Illus. Joseph Kelly

Perfect Snow
Barbara Reid, 2009

Picture a Tree
Barbara Reid, 2011

Please, Louise!
Frieda Wishinsky, 2007
Illus. Marie-Louise Gay

**A Pocket Can Have a
Treasure in It**
Kathy Stinson, 2008
Illus. Deirdre Betteridge

**Ready for Winter
(**and **Spring, Summer, Autumn)**
Marthe Jocelyn, 2008
(boardbook set of 4, by season)

The Red Wagon
Renata Liwska, 2011

**Roslyn Rutabaga and the
Biggest Hole on Earth!**
Marie-Louise Gay, 2010

Same Same
Marthe Jocelyn, 2009
Illus. Tom Slaughter

Shoe Shakes
Loris Lesynski, 2007
Illus. Michael Martchenko

**Sing a Song of
Mother Goose**
Barbara Reid, 2008

The Stone Hatchlings
Sarah Tsiang, 2012
Illus. Qin Leng

The Sweetest One of All
Jean Little, 2008
Illus. Marisol Sarrazin

Thing-Thing
Cary Fagan, 2008
Illus. Nicolas Debon

Time is When
Beth Gleick, 2008
Illus. Marthe Jocelyn

Toads on Toast
Linda Bailey, 2012
Illus. Colin Jack

A Visitor for Bear
Bonny Becker, 2008
Illus. Kady MacDonald Denton

**Welcome Song for Baby:
A Lullaby for Newborns**
Richard Van Camp, 2007

What Am I?
Linda Granfield, 2007
Illus. Jennifer Herbert

What Are You Doing?
Elisa Amado, 2011
Illus. Manuel Monroy

When Stella Was Very, Very Small
Marie-Louise Gay, 2009

Which Way?
Marthe Jocelyn, 2010
Illus. Tom Slaughter

Wiggle Giggle Tickle Train
Nora Hilb and
Sharon Jennings, 2009

Without You
Geneviève Côté, 2011

You're Mean, Lily Jean
Frieda Wishinsky, 2009
Illus. Kady MacDonald Denton

Storytime at the Library

These programs are for children birth to five years old and their parents or caregivers. They encourage a lifelong love of reading, build reading readiness in children, and show parents and caregivers how to help their child get ready for reading. All programs are free.

Baby Time
Bouncing and tickling rhymes, songs and stories for babies from birth to 18 months with their parents or caregivers.

Toddler Time
Stories, songs and rhymes for children age 19 months to 3 years with their parents or caregivers.

Preschool Time
Stories, songs and rhymes for children age 3 to 5 years with their parents or caregivers.

Family Time
Stories, songs, rhymes and activities for children age 5 and under with their parents or caregivers.

Pyjama Time
Bedtime stories, songs, rhymes and activities for children age 5 and under with their parents or caregivers.

torontopubliclibrary.ca/readyforreading

The books and CDs in this guide are only a few of the resources available at Toronto Public Library. Most books and CDs can help develop more than one Ready for Reading skill. Many books can be enjoyed by children of different ages.

Baby books

A You're Adorable
Buddy Kaye, Fred Wise and Sidney Lippman, 1994
Illus. Martha Alexander
This old song is brought to life with whimsical illustrations of children.

ABC x 3
♣ Marthe Jocelyn, 2005
Illus. Tom Slaughter
Simple illustrations and words, in three languages, introduce the letters of the alphabet to baby.

Baby Day
Susan Heyboer O'Keefe, 2006
Illus. Robin Spowart
Softly-coloured pictures show the activities which fill baby's day.

Baby Talk: A Book of First Words and Phrases
Judy Hindley, 2006
Illus. Bita Granström
Pictures of happy, energetic children and rhyming text show "a day in the life of a baby."

Big City Song
♣ Debora Pearson, 2006
Illus. Lynn Rowe Reed
The whole family will love the crazy sounds heard as they travel through the big city.

Big Fat Hen
Keith Baker, 1994
In this cute rhyming book, there are only a few words per page and the print is big and easy to see.

Brown Bear, Brown Bear, What Do You See?
Bill Martin, 1983
Illus. Eric Carle
Brown Bear meets up with an assortment of humorously coloured animal friends.

Busy Little Mouse
♣ Eugenie Fernandes, 2002
Illus. Kim Fernandes
A sweet and curious mouse leads the reader around a summertime farm, repeating and rhyming familiar words.

Clip-Clop
Nicola Smee, 2006
Mr. Horse is offering all of his barnyard friends a ride on his back. All is well until they fall off into a stack of hay.

Color Farm and Color Zoo
Lois Ehlert, 1990, 1989
Colours and shapes combine on cut-out pages to create images of different animals.

Daddy Hugs 1 2 3
Karen Katz, 2005
How many daddy hugs does baby want?

Daddy's Lullaby
Tony Bradman, 2001
Illus. Jason Cockcroft
Daddy sings the little one to sleep as they stroll through the house.

Five Little Ducks
Illus. Ivan Bates, 2006
You can choose to read or sing about the ducklings that went over the hills and far away.

Flora McDonnell's ABC
Flora McDonnell, 1997
This ABC book is full of colour and energy as it introduces young children to the world of words and letters, playfully and clearly.

Freight Train
Donald Crews, 1978
See all the colours of the rainbow as a brightly-coloured freight train rumbles along on a cross-country journey.

Goodnight Moon
Margaret Wise Brown, 1947
Illus. Clement Hurd
This classic book is perfect for bedtime. After sharing this story with your child, say goodnight to all the things around your child's bedroom.

Hickory Dickory Dock
Keith Baker, 2007
This familiar nursery rhyme is brought to life by this talented illustrator.

Hot Cold Shy Bold
❧ Pamela Harris, 1995
Faces abound in this classic collection of photos depicting opposites.

I Love You, Little One
Nancy Tafuri, 1998
Several baby animals ask, "Do you love me, Mama?" In every instance mothers reassure their babies that they are very much loved.

Night Cars
❧ Teddy Jam, 1988
Illus. Eric Beddows
"Once there was a baby/ Who wouldn't go to sleep." Thus begins this enchanting bedtime story about all the nighttime goings-on outside baby's window and one very tired dad.

No Matter What
Emma Dodd, 2007
Mama elephant will always love her baby… no matter what. This book told in rhyme will appeal to both babies and toddlers.

Over Under
❧ Marthe Jocelyn, 2005
Illus. Tom Slaughter
Bold shapes and primary colours complement this rhyming text. "Over, under, up and down." Playful opposites help introduce young children to new vocabulary.

Peekaboo Morning
Rachel Isadora, 2002
Who will the next peekaboo be…a bunny, a friend, grandma?

Peek-a-Little Boo
❧ Sheree Fitch, 2005
Illus. Laura Watson
Babies from around the world enjoy playing peek-a-boo in this rhyming alphabet book.

Peek-a-Moo!
Marie Torres Cimarusti, 1998
Illus. Stephanie Peterson
Play peek-a-boo with farm animals. This book is a fun choice for building print motivation because it has flaps that lift, simple, vibrant illustrations, and it invites kids to make animal sounds. Other titles by this author are: *Peek-a-Pet!*, *Peek-a-Boooo!* and *Peek-a-Zoo!*

The Runaway Bunny
Margaret Wise Brown, 1942
Illus. Clement Hurd
A little rabbit who wants to run away tells his mother how he will escape, but she is always right behind him in this comforting story of a bunny's imaginary game and the loving mother who finds him every time.

Ten Little Fingers and Ten Little Toes
Mem Fox, 2008
Illus. Helen Oxenbury
This delightful book celebrates a world of adorable babies.

Ten, Nine, Eight
Molly Bang, 1983
Counting back from ten, a young girl gets ready for bed. Simple comforting images of everyday things – shoes, a nightgown and a teddy bear – make this a classic bedtime story.

Ten Tiny Tickles
Karen Katz, 2005
Greet baby's day with tickles!

This New Baby
❧ Teddy Jam, 1998
Illus. Karen Reczuch
The joy of loving and caring for baby is beautifully portayed in this book that both baby and caregiver will enjoy.

Time for Bed
Mem Fox, 1993
Illus. Jane Dyer
The gentle language and soothing rhythm of the words put animals and little ones to sleep at the end of the day.

Toot Toot Beep Beep
Emma Garcia, 2008
Kids will have fun making the sounds of the many colourful cars on this trip until they're all quiet in the parking lot.

Welcome, Precious
Nikki Grimes, 2006
Illus. Bryan Collier
Introduce your baby to the joy and satisfaction that reading together can bring to the whole family.

What Will We Do with the Baby-O?
♣ Theo Heras, 2004
Illus. Jennifer Herbert
This children's librarian's collection of songs and action rhymes for babies is an invaluable tool for every parent.

Where's Spot?
Eric Hill, 1980
Lift the flaps to find Spot's hiding place.

Who's That Baby?: New-Baby Songs
Sharon Creech, 2005
Illus. David Diaz
A collection of baby songs by a Newbery Award-winning author.

Check your local library for titles in board book format by Byron Barton, Sandra Boynton, Lucy Cousins, Karen Katz, Tana Hoban, Marthe Jocelyn and Jonathan London.

Toddler books

AlphaBEEP
♣ Debora Pearson, 2003
Illus. Edward Miller
The whole family will love this alphabet book as it depicts vehicles from ambulance to zamboni.

At a Construction Site
♣ Don Kilby, 2003
This non-fiction book shows the demolition of an old building and the construction of a new one.

B is for Bulldozer: A Construction ABC
June Sobel, 2003
Illus. Melissa Iwai
What are all those mighty machines busy building?

Bee-bim Bop!
Linda Sue Park, 2005
Illus. Ho Baek Lee
A little girl helps her mother shop for and prepare a favourite meal of delicious Bee-bim Bop.

Building with Dad
Carol Nevius, 2006
Illus. Bill Thomson
The team builds a new school. Watch the machinery at work!

The Carrot Seed
Ruth Krauss, 1945
Illus. Crockett Johnson
Use this classic about a little boy who patiently waits for his seed to sprout to promote narrative skills.

Chicka Chicka Boom Boom
Bill Martin, Jr. and John Archambault, 1989
Illus. Lois Ehlert
Everyone can participate in this classic which features bold illustrations of letters falling from a coconut tree and a rhythmic chant. Check your local library branch to find a copy of Bill Martin's board book called Chicka Chicka ABC.

Cleo's Alphabet Book
Stella Blackstone, 2003
Illus. Caroline Mockford
Brightly illustrated objects allow Cleo the cat to introduce toddlers to the alphabet.

Dear Zoo
Rod Campbell, 1982
If you wrote to the zoo asking for a pet, what would they send you? There are clues on the boxes in this lift-the-flap book.

Digger Man
Andrea Zimmerman and David Clemesha, 2003
Colourful little diggers scoop and dump as they build a playground in the park.

Dim Sum for Everyone!
Grace Lin, 2001
At a dim sum restaurant, a family picks their favourite dishes from steaming trolleys.

Dinosaur Roar!
Paul and Henrietta Stickland, 1994
This colourful rhyming book of opposites introduces all sorts of dinosaurs as they head for lunch.

Dinosnores
Kelly DiPucchio, 2005
Illus. Ponder Goembel
Tongue-twisting rhymes make this book fun to read aloud.

Eyes, Nose, Fingers, and Toes: A First Book All about You
Judy Hindley, 1999
Illus. Brita Granström
It's fun to learn the names of all the parts of your body.

First the Egg
Laura Vaccaro Seeger, 2007
Starting with the lovely oval of an egg, cut-out pages draw attention to all kinds of different shapes.

Five Little Chicks
Nancy Tafuri, 2006
Five chicks and their mother peck in the corn patch in search of breakfast.

Five Little Monkeys Jumping on the Bed
Eileen Christelow, 1989
Mother calls the doctor after her five naughty monkeys fall off the bed and bump their heads.

Go Away, Big Green Monster!
Ed Emberley, 1992
This book uses simple shapes and bright colours. Each page features a new part of a big green monster, which then disappears one part at a time as the children participate and command it to go away.

Good Night Sam
✤ Marie-Louise Gay, 2003
Stella and Sam face scary corners of the house at night, while searching for sneaky Fred the dog. Will Sam ever get to sleep?

Hand, Hand, Fingers, Thumb
Al Perkins, 1969
Illus. Eric Gurney
A bouncy rhyming text makes counting fingers and thumbs lots of fun.

Here Comes Mother Goose
Iona Opie, 1999
Illus. Rosemary Wells
Opie and Wells team up to create a wonderful collection of Mother Goose rhymes.

I Can Do It Too!
Karen Baicker, 2003
Illus. Ken Wilson-Max
Your child will love the idea of doing and helping and you will love the large clear print.

I Like Black and White
Barbara Jean Hicks, 2006
Illus. Lila Prap
Toddlers will want to hear this brightly illustrated rhyming concept book again and again.

It Looked Like Spilt Milk
Charles G. Shaw, 1947
Fourteen white shapes on a deep blue background portray familiar and less familiar objects.

Kitten's First Full Moon
Kevin Henkes, 2004
Poor Kitten, she just cannot reach that delectable-looking bowl of milk she sees high up in the sky.

Mama's Day
Linda Ashman, 2006
Illus. Jan Ormerod
A list of all the tender things mothers do for their little ones. Perfect for bedtime reading.

The Mighty Street Sweeper
Patrick Moore, 2006
Truck lovers will enjoy comparing and contrasting the little street sweeper to other powerful trucks. Colourful illustrations and informative text.

Mouse Shapes
Ellen Stoll Walsh, 2007
Look what three little mice can make with the shapes they find!

Mr. Gumpy's Outing
John Burningham, 1970
The animals want to have a ride in Mr. Gumpy's boat, but will they all fit?

My Big Boy Bed
Eve Bunting, 2003
Illus. Maggie Smith
A little boy gleefully tells why he loves his new big boy bed.

No, David!
David Shannon, 1998
The large print in this book makes it very clear what David should not do.

On Mother's Lap
Ann Herbert Scott, 1992
Illus. Glo Coalson
There is always room for one more on Mother's lap in this gentle story set in the far north.

Peace at Last
Jill Murphy, 1980
Mr. Bear just can't get to sleep – the night is full of noises.

Rosie's Walk
Pat Hutchins, 1968
Rosie the hen goes for a walk through the barnyard. Who is following her?

Round is a Mooncake
Roseanne Thong, 2000
Illus. Grace Lin
Picking out the shapes of objects in this book is an excellent beginning step to letter knowledge.

The Seals on the Bus
Lenny Hort, 2000
Illus. G. Brian Karas
Here is the familiar song with a fun twist, as more and more animals come to ride the bus.

The Sleepy Little Alphabet: A Bedtime Story from Alphabet Town
Judy Sierra, 2009
Illus. Melissa Sweet
Alphabet letters get ready for bed. Upper case letters are parents, and the children are lower case.

Sleepytime Kittens
Joanne Partis, 2005
Review the numbers one to ten along with three bouncy kittens.

Snow
✤ Joan Clark, 2006
Illus. Kady MacDonald Denton
Snow is everywhere and it has Sammy wondering about what lies beneath the snow banks.

This Little Chick
John Lawrence, 2002
Play with all the different animal noises as little chick walks around the barnyard. The simple, repetitive rhyme can be sung to the tune of *Five Little Ducks*. Ask your child to make the animal sounds.

Tiger
Nick Butterworth, 2006
A baby kitten pretends he is a real tiger with "great, big, tiger claws!" and "a loud, scary, tiger ROAR!"

To Market, To Market
Anne Miranda, 1997
Illus. Janet Stevens
This old lady has a very strange shopping list that starts with a pig.

Toot and Puddle: Puddle's ABC
Holly Hobbie, 2000
A wonderful alphabet book for Toot and Puddle fans.

The Very Hungry Caterpillar
Eric Carle, 1969
A very hungry caterpillar nibbles on everything from salami to lollipops as it eats its way through the pages of this whimsical and wholly irresistible book.

What Do You Do with a Tail Like This?
Steve Jenkins, 2003
Illus. Robin Page
This is a wonderful book for those who love non-fiction. Read all about amazing and weird animal body parts.

The Wheels on the Bus
Paul O. Zelinsky, 1990
One of many adaptations of this cheerful song.

Where Is the Green Sheep?
Mem Fox, 2004
Illus. Judy Horacek
Our green sheep must be here, somewhere… Let's look!

Where's My Darling Daughter?
Mij Kelly, 2005
Illus. Katharine McEwen
Silly Daddy searches for his little girl high and low in a farmyard setting.

Whose Mouse are You?
Robert Kraus, 1970
Illus. Jose Aruego
A lonely little mouse has to be resourceful in order to bring his family back together.

Yo, Baby
✤ Roslyn Schwartz, 2002
Toddlers will have lots of fun trying to figure out the identity of each mystery object.

Preschooler books

Actual Size
Steve Jenkins, 2004
This engaging non-fiction book introduces children to some of the wonders of our natural world.

Alligator Pie
✤ Dennis Lee, 1974
Illus. Frank Newfeld
This poetry book is a true classic of Canadian children's literature.

Alphabet Under Construction
Denise Fleming, 2002
Mouse is hard at work constructing his way through the alphabet with activities that begin with each letter of the alphabet.

AlphaBETTER
✤ Dan Bar-el, 2006
Illus. Graham Ross
One letter leads to the next, but not necessarily in any way that makes sense.

Are You My Mother?
P.D. Eastman, 1960
A little bird falls out of its nest, and looks everywhere for its mother.

Bear Snores On
Karma Wilson, 2002
Illus. Jane Chapman
Bear sleeps while more and more animals enter his cave to escape the cold weather outside. He's missing all the fun!

Ben Over Night
✤ Sarah Ellis, 2005
Illus. Kim LaFave
Homesickness makes it hard for this preschooler to have sleepovers with his friend.

Big, Bigger, Biggest!
Nancy Coffelt, 2009
After reading this colourful book your vocabulary will be jumbo, gigantic, colossal!

Chester
✤ Mélanie Watt, 2007
Who's writing this book anyway? Author Mélanie Watt begins to tell the story of a mouse, but Chester takes over.

City Signs
✤ Zoran Milich, 2002
Look at all the words that you can see as you go through the city!

Click Clack Moo: Cows that Type
Doreen Cronin, 2000
Illus. Betsy Lewin
When the cows find a typewriter in the barn, Farmer Brown's problems begin.

Corduroy
Don Freeman, 1968
A little bear in a toy shop wishes for nothing more than a friend to take him home.

Daddy Goes To Work
Jabari Asim, 2006
Illus. Aaron Boyd
Follow this little one as she goes to work with her daddy.

Drumheller Dinosaur Dance
✤ Robert Heidbreder, 2004
Illus. Bill Slavin, Esperança Melo
By daylight, the Drumheller dinosaurs rest their ancient bones. But when the moon rises, so do these slumbering skeletons.

Eating the Alphabet: Fruits & Vegetables from A to Z
Lois Ehlert, 1989
There is something to eat for every letter of the alphabet and it all looks delicious.

Eddie Longpants
✤ Mireille Levert, 2005
Children will love the story of tall Eddie who shows everyone that being big is not so bad after all.

The End
David LaRochelle, 2007
Illus. Richard Egielski
Those who like to skip to the ending will love this book which ends with the beginning.

The Enormous Potato
✦ Aubrey Davis, 1998
Illus. Dušan Petričić
A cumulative tale about a farmer who wants to harvest his vegetable.

Every Friday
Dan Yaccarino, 2007
A sweet and simple story about father-son bonding. An ideal book for sharing.

Fancy Nancy
Jane O'Connor, 2006
Illus. Robin Priess Glasser
Why be plain when you can be fancy? Vocabulary is "fancy" for words.

Franklin in the Dark
✦ Paulette Bourgeois, 1986
Illus. Brenda Clark
It's dark inside Franklin's turtle shell and it's scary!

The Gingerbread Girl
Lisa Campbell Ernst, 2006
Gingerbread girls rule in this amusing re-telling of the classic tale.

Harry the Dirty Dog
Gene Zion, 1956
Illus. Margaret Bloy Graham
After a day playing outside, Harry changes from a white dog with black spots, to a black dog with white spots.

Henny Penny
✦ H. Werner Zimmermann, 1989
Funny illustrations will make children laugh as the birds rush to tell the king that the sky is falling.

Josias, Hold the Book
Jennifer Riesmeyer Elvgren, 2006
Illus. Nicole Tadgell
Josias' beans are not growing, but he scoffs at the idea of consulting a book to solve the problem.

Kenya's Word
Linda Trice, 2006
Illus. Pamela Johnson
Kenya has a hard time choosing her favourite describing word, but finally picks one that encompasses all of her favourite things.

The Little Old Lady Who Was not Afraid of Anything
Linda Williams, 1986
Illus. Megan Lloyd
Who knows who you will meet on a dark Halloween night!

The Little Red Hen
Paul Galdone, 1973
None of the Red Hen's friends will help her plant the seeds or harvest the wheat, but they all want a piece of the cake she makes from the flour.

Llama Llama Red Pajama
Anna Dewdney, 2005
After being tucked into bed by his mother, baby llama doesn't want to be left alone. This reassuring tale is told in rhyme.

Lola at the Library
Anna McQuinn, 2006
Illus. Rosalind Beardshaw
On Tuesdays, Lola goes to the library with her mother.

The Mitten: A Ukrainian Folk Tale
Jan Brett, 1989
A beautifully illustrated version of the traditional story about animals who take shelter in a lost mitten.

The Napping House
Audrey Wood, 1984
Illus. Don Wood
One rainy day, everyone is asleep in the big cosy bed, except for one little flea.

The New Girl…and Me
Jacqui Robbins, 2006
Illus. Matt Phelan
This is a gentle story of making friends and fitting in. Mia uses books to find a way to break the ice with her new classmate Shakeeta.

On Your Toes: A Ballet ABC
Rachel Isadora, 2003
A ballet company dances across the pages of this sparkling picture book, inviting you behind the scenes and illuminating ballet terms from A to Z.

Only a Cow
✦ Arlene Hamilton, 2006
Illus. Dean Griffiths
Lucille may only be a cow, but she has the heart of a racehorse.

✦ Canadian

Paper Bag Princess
✤ Robert Munsch, 1980
Illus. Michael Martchenko
When a dragon burns her clothes and captures her fiancé, Princess Elizabeth is forced to wear a paper bag and engage the dragon in a battle of wits.

Red is Best
✤ Kathy Stinson, 1982
Illus. Robin Baird Lewis
No one understands the perfection of red like this little girl.

Roar of a Snore
✤ Marsha Diane Arnold, 2006
Illus. Pierre Pratt
While each and every other Huffle is asleep, little Jack is awakened by a tremendous snore.

A Sea-Wishing Day
✤ Robert Heidbreder, 2007
Illus. Kady MacDonald Denton
A wish plus a vivid imagination equals a pirate adventure.

A Second is a Hiccup: A Child's Book of Time
✤ Hazel Hutchins, 2004
Illus. Kady MacDonald Denton
Any parent who's been asked how long a minute is, or any child who's wondered what an hour means will enjoy this smart, simple book.

Slugs in Love
Susan Pearson, 2006
Illus. Kevin O'Malley
Two young slugs leave messages for each other throughout the farmyard.

Sofie and the City
Karima Grant, 2006
Illus. Janet Montecalvo
Sofie is missing the beauty of her birth place, Senegal. It isn't until she makes a new friend and is able to alter her bleak surroundings that she begins to feel some peace in her new city.

Something from Nothing: Adapted from a Jewish Folktale
✤ Phoebe Gilman, 1992
In this retelling of a Jewish folktale, a child's grandfather transforms a worn-out blanket into a jacket. What happens when the jacket wears out?

Sophie and the Sea Monster
✤ Don Gillmor, 2005
Illus. Michael Martchenko
Sophie and a sea monster face their fears together by going on all sorts of adventures.

Swimmy
Leo Lionni, 1968
Deep in the sea a happy school of little fish is afraid to come out of hiding . . . until Swimmy comes along.

Ten Sly Piranhas: A Counting Story in Reverse (A Tale of Wickedness and Worse!)
William Wise, 1993
Illus. Victoria Chess
Ten piranhas diminish, "with a gulp and a gurgle," to one, and that one also comes to a sorry but satisfying end.

Three Billy Goats Gruff
Paul Galdone, 1973
In this traditional tale, three goats want to visit the green pasture on the other side of the river, but a fearsome troll guards the bridge.

The Turn-Around, Upside-Down Alphabet Book
Lisa Campbell Ernst, 2004
Not your run-of-the-mill alphabet book. Your preschooler will love this one.

A Very Unusual Dog
✤ Dorothy Joan Harris, 2004
Illus. Kim LaFave
Jonathan has a very unusual dog that only he can see.

Wake Up, Henry Rooster!
✤ Margriet Ruurs, 2006
Illus. Sean Cassidy
Poor Henry is not a morning rooster, but when his father is called out of town, the responsibility of waking the entire farm rests on his sleepy feathers.

We're Going on a Bear Hunt
Michael Rosen, 1989
Illus. Helen Oxenbury
Brave hunters must overcome many
obstacles before they find the fierce bear
in its cave.

When Daddy's Truck Picks Me Up
Jana Novotny Hunter, 2006
Illus. Carol Thompson
The best part of this little one's day is
when Daddy arrives in his big red truck.

*When Sophie Gets Angry –
Really, Really Angry…*
Molly Bang, 1999
Everyone feels angry sometimes. The
illustrations brilliantly capture Sophie's
changing emotions.

When You Were Small
♣ Sara O'Leary, 2006
Illus. Julie Morstad
When a son demands, "Tell me about
when I was small," his father shares a
variety of sweet and humorous
memories.

The Wonderful Pigs of Jillian Jiggs
♣ Phoebe Gilman, 1988
"Jillian, Jillian, Jillian Jiggs" makes
oodles of cloth pigs to sell but she gets
so attached to each stuffed animal that
she can't part with any of them. What
will she do?

You Can't Rush a Cat
Karleen Bradford, 2003
Illus. Leslie Elizabeth Watts
With quiet patience and a clever plan,
Jessica helps her Granddaddy lure a
stray cat indoors.

Z is for Zamboni: A Hockey Alphabet
♣ Matt Napier, 2002
Illus. Melanie Rose
Rhyming text highlights many aspects of
hockey, one for each letter of the
alphabet.

Books for parents, caregivers and professionals

*Baby Read-Aloud Basics: Fun and
interactive ways to help your little
one discover the world of words*
Caroline J. Blakemore and Barbara
Weston Ramirez, 2006

*♣ I'm a Little Teapot!: Presenting
preschool storytime*
Jane Cobb, comp., 1996
Illus. Magda Lazicka

*The Complete Idiot's Guide to
Reading with Your Child*
Helen Coronato, 2007

*Play & Learn: 1001 fun activities for
your baby and child*
Susan Elisabeth Davis and Nancy Wilson
Hall, 2008

*Early Learning for Every Child Today:
A framework for Ontario early
childhood settings*
Best Start Expert Panel on Early
Learning, 2007

*Every Child Ready to Read: Literacy
tips for parents*
The Lee Pesky Learning Center, 2004

*Reading Magic: Why reading aloud
to our children will change their
lives forever*
Mem Fox, 2001

*Early Literacy Storytimes @ Your
Library: Partnering with caregivers
for success*
Saroj Nadkarni Ghoting, 2006

*♣ Where are the Stars: A treasury of
interactive rhymes*
Celia Barker Lottridge, Glenna Janzen
and Carol Leigh Wehking, comps., 2006

Reading Activities A-Z
Joanne Matricardi and Jeanne McLarty,
2008

*A Parent's Guide to Reading with
Your Young Child*
Susan B. Neuman and Tanya S. Wright,
2007

*The Complete Idiot's Guide to Baby
Brain Games: Over 200 brain-
boosting games for brilliant babies*
Lawrence E. Shapiro and Jennifer Lawler,
2008

Reading Games for Young Children
Jackie Silberg, 2005

*Bright from the Start: The simple,
science-backed way to nurture your
child's developing mind, from birth
to age 3*
Jill Stamm, 2007

The Read-Aloud Handbook, 6th ed.
Jim Trelease, 2006

Music CDs by artist

❋ **Barenaked Ladies**
Snack Time!

Laurie Berkner
- *The Best of the Laurie Berkner Band*
- *Under a Shady Tree*

❋ **Charlotte Diamond**
10 Carrot Diamond

❋ **Jack Grunsky**
My Beautiful World

❋ **Sally Jaeger**
Lullabies & Laprhymes

Ella Jenkins
Early, Early Childhood Songs

Bob McGrath
- *The Baby Record*
- *Songs and Games for Toddlers*

❋ **Michael & Jello**
It Must be Jelly, 'cause Jam Don't Shake

Hap Palmer
- *Early Childhood Classics*
- *Hap Palmer Sings Classic Nursery Rhymes*

❋ **Fred Penner**
The Cat Came Back

❋ **Raffi**
- *Everything Grows*
- *More Singable Songs for the Very Young*
- *Singable Songs for the Very Young*

❋ **Kathy Reid-Naiman**
- *More Tickles & Tunes*
- *A Smooth Road to London Town*

❋ **Sharon, Lois & Bram**
- *Great Big Hits*
- *One Elephant, Deux Eléphants*

❋ **Mike Whitla**
Early Morning Knee-Slappin' Tunes

❋ **The Wiggles**
Let's Eat!

Recommended websites

❋ **ABC Life Literacy**
ABC Life Literacy Canada is a non-profit organization that inspires Canadians to increase their literacy skills. Visit this site for the latest news and information on family literacy, research and programs.
abclifeliteracy.ca

❋ **Canadian Children's Book Centre**
The Centre promotes and supports Canadian books with programs, publications, resources and more.
bookcentre.ca

Every Child Ready to Read
The American Library Association website includes a review of the research upon which the Every Child Ready to Read program is based.
everychildreadytoread.org

❋ **Ontario Ministry of Education**
Helping your child learn to read – A parent's guide.
edu.gov.on.ca/eng/document/ brochure/earlyreading/index.html

❋ **Mothercraft/CITYKIDS**
CITYKIDS is a network of agencies working together to coordinate services to children with special needs and their families. It serves children from birth to 6 years and children from 6 to 12 years attending daycare, who reside in the greater Toronto area.
mothercraft.ca/index. php?q=citykids

Reading Rockets: Launching Young Readers
Parents can find tips to help turn their young children into readers.
pbs.org/launchingreaders

❋ **Toronto Preschool Speech and Language Services**
Toronto Preschool Speech and Language Services are free and also available in French to qualifying infants, toddlers, preschool children and their families living in Toronto experiencing challenges with communication development, hearing loss and visual impairment.
tpsls.on.ca

❋ **Toronto Public Health**
Find information about child development, nutrition, child safety and resources for parents.
toronto.ca/health

❋ **Toronto Public Library**
Good tips for parents on raising readers and choosing the right books for young children.
torontopubliclibrary.ca/ readyforreading

Zero to Three
A wealth of information about the behaviour and development of children in their early years.
zerotothree.org

TD Summer Reading Club

TD Summer Reading Club helps keep kids reading, all summer long. Sign up at your local branch and enjoy free programs, games, crafts, activities and more.

tdsummerreadingclub.ca

Developed by

In partnership with

Title sponsor

Commitment to literacy

Every parent wants his child to succeed. Compelling studies show that to succeed in school, a child needs to be literate, and that children begin to learn literacy skills as soon as they are born, long before they enter school. Toronto Public Library, a leader in early literacy services in the community, has modelled *Ready for Reading* on the American Library Association's initiative *Every Child Ready to Read @ the Library*. Both are library-based programs that enlist parents and caregivers as key players in promoting early childhood literacy, giving them the information and the tools they need to help their children acquire the necessary skills.

Every Child Ready to Read and Toronto Public Library's *Ready for Reading* are founded on research into areas as diverse as national literacy statistics, school readiness studies, stages of brain development and early childhood development.

Literacy

Despite Canada's standing in the world as a rich and educated nation, adult literacy is a persistent problem. Statistics show that more than 48% of all Canadian adults do not have the literacy skills required to cope in a modern society. This means that they have difficulty reading, understanding and functioning effectively with written material.[1]

School readiness

Research shows that an astonishing number of children are ill-prepared for school. The groundwork for success is laid in the home. Simple practices such as reading daily with a child and making books available in the home can counteract potentially negative factors such as low socio-economic status. The relationship between the skills with which children enter school and their later academic performance is striking. Children who start school without the necessary skills typically stay behind.

Brain development in early childhood

Scientists have found that the architecture of the brain develops in stages beginning before birth, and each stage of development builds on the previous one. In the first years of life, connections between brain synapses are made at an astounding rate. At the same time, there are windows of opportunity which are optimal periods for acquiring language and other skills. It is important, therefore, that during the early years children are given the physical, emotional and social support they need that will allow the brain to develop to its full potential. Children raised in nurturing and stimulating environments build the neural pathways that support healthy development.[2]

Literacy in early childhood

Researchers continue to investigate all aspects of early childhood literacy. In recent years, research has focussed on trying to measure the connection between acquiring pre-emergent literacy skills and later literacy success. In addition, once the importance of a particular skill has been recognized, the best ways to teach that skill are being studied. Many of the latest findings focus on the effects of experience on brain development, and in particular, on the value of play as a way of learning skills.

As new information comes forward, Toronto Public Library continues to make adjustments to its *Ready for Reading* programs based on the research.

Ready for Reading programs are built on these principles:

- Parents and caregivers are a child's first and best teachers, and the home is where the child begins to learn.

- Communication begins at birth.

- The parent-child relationship is the basis of the child's success.

- Parents and caregivers will benefit from knowing about their child's stages of development in language and literacy.

- Children learn through play.

- The library supports and complements what families can do at home.

[1] OECD, *International Adult Literacy and Skills Survey*, http://www.ccl-cca.ca/CCL/Reports/ReadingFuture.html

[2] Margaret McCain, Fraser Mustard and Stuart Shanker, *Early Years Study 2: Putting science into action*, 2007

It's time to get a library card!

With a **free** library card, you and your child can borrow
picture books, **audiobooks**, kids' magazines,
music and **movies** to enjoy together.

Visit any library branch to get your child,
and yourself, a free library card today.

All kids
belong at the library.

The library welcomes children with
special needs and their families.

**Ask us how some of our
programs can be adapted.**

Call Answerline: 416-393-7131
TTY: 416-393-7030

torontopubliclibrary.ca